# The Shadow on the Wall of Your Mind
A look at the Other side of teenage depression

By
Kate Ringland and Ellie Ringland

Copyright © 2006 by Kate Ringland and Ellie Ringland.

All Rights Reserved.

No portion of this book may be copied without written permission from the authors.

Published by Ringland Publishing. Seattle, WA. 2006.

ISBN: 978-0-6151-3771-1

Cover Photograph: "Sammamish River by Night" © 2006 by Kate Ringland.

Interior Portraits and Back Cover Portrait © 2006 by Ellie Ringland.

For Becky, who oozes optimism out of every pore

And

For my cousin and Co. author, Kate, for her love and support in everything I've wanted and accomplished in my life

## Acknowledgments

We would like to thank everyone who has supported us in the creation and editing of this book. We couldn't have done it without you.

A special thanks goes to our grandmother, Elinor Ringland. You have helped us see the world in a new and better light. Our "secret meeting" on the lawn gave us a new perspective and will be a cherished memory forever. Without your love and encouragement, this book may never have reached its full potential. Thank you.

-Much Love, Kate & Ellie

I would also like to thank my mother for reaching out to me. Looking back, I see nothing to regret and I remember only the happiest times. Thank you to my father for giving me your talent for organization and always being able to make me laugh. There are no words to express my gratitude for all you both have given me.

Love, Your Katydid

There are also two special people in my life I'd like to thank. These people have helped me grow and change in ways they'll never know. They were on my side when no one else was. I would not be the better person I am today without them.

Love Infinity, Ellie

## Contents

PART I.

    By Ellie Ringland............................................... 9

PART II.

    By Kate Ringland.............................................. 35

# PART I.

Looking through the lenses of a teenager with depression.

By Ellie Ringland

# Introduction

Having a problem like depression, bipolar disorder, anxiety, or any other mental illness is not fun or glamorous. Usually, you don't want the attention you get. You can't get out of bed because you think all your friends hate you or skip a whole day of school because you have to be in a socially uncomfortable situation, like something awkward or embarrassing. This is not being able to function.

No one wants to feel this way. Most people that are depressed just want to be "normal" or just want to be able to get out of bed in the morning. Small things can seem huge. Imagine you're walking down the hall and someone laughs, suddenly you feel like everyone is laughing at you. Normal situations can be altered into something bigger or harder than it could possibly be.

It's hard for a lot of people, especially with anxiety or depression, to actually have a normal conversation with people. Talking about feelings or even everyday stuff can be terrifying. For some people, like me, writing has made a big impact on that fear. When my mind is full and my thoughts are racing, sometimes when I write it down, it can help me figure things out. I've stopped running from my problems; and when there's nothing else, I can still write.

-Ellie Ringland

No longer needing this
No longer i wait for this
I give in to this
Silent rooms fill my head
Stretching roads to nowhere
Lead my walk
So what if you never heard me laugh
I grab for this
Holding for this dear life.

~

With no mouth i stay silent
to wait for a flood to wash it away
i give it all up
there is nothing here to give away
I'm empty
screaming with no voice
my body twists
it cracks
it breaks
it dies.

~

Wounded and burned
i take a blade with acid
it burns me through
it bleeds and wounds
i don't have a mind
i'm silent without face.
Wounded and burned
this is all fucked
it'll never change
this pain
it'll never fade
this scream
i keep inside
it'll burn me whole inside
it pulls the tears
to the surface
this wounds and burns.

~

Hello, Goodbye,

do you see me standing there,

still waiting for you,

alone without a peace of mind.

Tearing my body apart,

pulling out my broken heart.

My mind is quiet,

i don't have thoughts to sort through,

I'm without wanting,

needing,

feeling the empty space,

it fills up with cold,

the silence of the things i never say.

Free of mind and heart,

i drift away,

unworried of this consequence,

unwounded, and bleeding by your unwanted knife.

Morning, Evening,

i'm alone, but its okay,

the tears in my eyes froze and turned to ice,

it holds me down,

makes me numb.

Goodnight,

for the last time,

i fold into the darkness,

let it take me down,

let me be dark and weightless with it,

without this.

~

Slowly but surely,
it sucks me dry,
my lungs burn up inside,
without moving in any direction,
it pulls me out,
then pulls me down,
takes my life and breaks my heart,
it burns me down,
it drowns me out.
Seeping through all the cracks,
it finds its way,
into my heart,
it knows my faults,
my loves,
my cuts,
it breaks me down and sucks me dry.

~

This is my freak,

this is my tear,

my times to scream,

alone in fear.

I need you here, someone to help me through,

as i lay awake at night,

i dream of things that take this pain.

No one wants me around,

im ignored to the core,

im always listening,

to what you have to say,

i didn't do a god damn thing,

maybe its better off this way,

cover your eyes and turn away from me.

This is my freak,

my tear,

to be here is a chore,

i think its my time to die,

its time to get that bottle of monoxide.

Still i search for a reason,

someone please give me a reason,

to breathe that extra breath,

just after death has passed me by.

~

This drug,
this drink,
this pill.
Without them i am drowning,
i slip into a dream,
its there constantly,
eating away at me.
You know you want the little pill,
it helps you sleep at night.
The drink that cures you of depression,
even if its only for a little while.
The drug expands your mind,
you think beyond this wall we've built.
It holds you down,
pulls and twists,
your fingers burn,
rips you into something worthless.

~

I teeter on the edge,
this breaking point my mind,
it kills me inside to know that i'm the only one who knows,
i'm sinking so dangerously low,
on this unstable bridge,
sometimes i think it would be easier,
to just let it all give way.
~

The fire burns,

it makes me hot and tired,

i want to hold you close to me,

i want you deep inside my burning fire,

i crawl away,

to rip into myself,

i hate myself,

i won't let you see me blue,

trying to ignore all the feelings the suck me down to drown,

if i let you see my every lie,

if you saw me scream just like i want to,

i'd shake my walls and crack this mirror

that stares back into me,

the fire burns me up inside,

i fucking hate you ,

i fucking hate me,

i fucking hate everything,

you never did for me.

~

Held me down,
pushing me deep into the ground,
your breath is shallow,
my tears are cold.
You bind my wrists,
till they're numb and white.
You hold me down,
pushing my face into the carpet,
i feel the scream burn in my throat,
i feel my stomach stir.
I lie still,
i lie broken,
you breathe a sigh,
you lift your weight away.
Turn and leave my hell you've created,
"don't say a word"
floats back to me.
My tears are dried,
i lie still,
i lie broken,
i wont move an inch,
i fear to move at all,
for i'll shatter into pieces,
i lie still i lie broken,
i lie,
letting your memory have its way with me.

~

Love is my heroin,
lifts me up so high,
i'll do anything i can,
to keep me seeing life this way.
Love is my heroin,
makes me feel so low,
so i won't feel a thing,
if i end everything.
Love is my drug of choice,
love is my fucked up medication.
It'll make me laugh,
to make me cry.
Love is my drug of choice,
lifts me high,
drags me low,
love is the only way to go.

~

Bodies intertwined,
under a hormone driven sky,
lovers lying close,
in a bed of dying roses,
shaking for one kiss,
as your lips brush over mine,
whisper nothings sweet,
your smile melts me to tears,
then you turn your back on me.

~

Talk talk talk,
open up and scream,
disgusted looks,
as they fade away from me,
shadows play with my mind,
tease my fate,
pulling me away,
making it all unreal.
Talk talk talk,
open up and scream,
turn your back,
running from pain,
dropping down to die,
leaving me sucked dry,
weightless,
pale,
breaking apart,
just fly.
Talk talk talk,
open up,
just scream,
let me get it out,
hold me right,
tightly,
just breathe.

~

take my hand, but not my heart,
lead me through,
all this blue i'm going through.
You break my heart with your eyes,
i see them die,
i see them cry,
i feel a pull to you,
it drowns me.
Take my hand, but never my heart,
it's been dropped and thrown,
pricked and torn, then glued and sewn.
My hand is sore along with my heart,
don't touch me now,
i just need a place to let it all fall apart.

~

The walls keep tripping,
Everything melts away.
My screams just echo,
Bounce into the distance,
Fall into oblivion.
The body is melting,
Suspended,
I blend into the scenery.
~

It lurks,

creeps up inside,

brings me down,

don't have a choice,

it burns,

paper cuts to the heart,

hold my breath,

it won't spread.

It sees,

i can do no good,

i will fail,

trip and fall.

it comes over me,

the shadow, it touches me,

holding my head above water,

i bring you down with me.

I won't change you,
can't change me,
take you away.
No, no, no,
it's all a blur,
can't see your face anymore.
Isn't this just where you wanted me,
said I'd never be,
these things don't change,
i'm the only one to blame.

I'm the one you pass over,
The one you don't need but keep for pleasure,
It burns me up but I sit and wait,
It doesn't matter because you're there in my mind,
Always yelling all the time,
It won't change; I'm indifferent,
Or so I try
To bury my feelings alive,
But you sit and wait for all my tears to wash away,
You lurk, a memory in my mind,
It will fade,
Or so I hope,
It doesn't matter, or so I wish.

Not good enough,
Sullen and alone,
Past the breaking point,
I descend.
I'm destroyed,
Inside out I'm burning,
Without you.
I'm seeing life is ruined,
I'm seeing my mistakes,
I made choices,
I made errors.
I ruined this,
Stupid stupid stupid girl,
It doesn't matter,
I'm fine I'm fine I'm fine.
Not good enough,
For anyone,
So alone,
But it's my fault,
I hate you,
Because I love you,
Don't let me ruin another.

This piece im missing,
this release i drive for,
my scream, it kills them,
the nails scrape til bone,
and i,
fall all into shards.

I wrap myself in a blanket,
To hide from all the sounds I created,
I break the love I needed,
Is it what I want?
Is it what I need?
They all scream at me now,
I've broken them all down,
I'm getting closer to the bottom,
As we speak, my lungs are heavy,
Breathing smoke,
Without air I need a release,
The walls are too small for my rage,
I hold it in,
All in,
To keep them safe,
But I can feel the hold shifting,
The cracks it's seeping through,
I can feel it burning,
It's not my fault when they get too close.

I don't need you, but I'd bleed for you,
Now this life will go unfinished,
And I just wish you could see how much you've affected me,
My feelings burn like fire,
Soaking through my skin,
I toss and turn and think of you,
There's nothing I can do.

# PART II.

Two sides to the coin, looking through the lenses of a teen with bipolar disorder.

By Kate Ringland

# Introduction

Mental illness can be a scary and lonely experience. Being a teenager with bipolar disorder can be an ordeal. Teenagers are already stressed with the burden of puberty, fitting in with their peers, and doing well in school to prepare for that ominous thing called the "future." Add the pain of depression and uncontrolled anxiety that comes with mania and you have one overwhelmed teenager.

Teenagers may feel alone, like there is no one else in the universe who feels the way they do. I didn't realize until my freshman year in college that everyone else has these same feelings. I believe parents and mentors are key in alleviating this feeling of aloneness. Adults should come to their teenager to talk to them as equals. A person who is depressed does not want to be patronized or looked down upon. They want kindness, understanding, and, most of all, to be reminded that eventually the pain will stop and life will be ok. Teenagers survive high school, grow up, and go on to be successful, *normal* people with jobs and families. The most important thing is to open the door of communication, be honest, and trust each other.

Looking back at my high school years, I can safely say I was triumphant. Through my disorder I found my voice in writing. Writing gave me the ability to sort through my own emotions and find hope for the future. I have chosen the following poems as my favorite gems from a large pile of treasures I produced during my high school years. When first writing these poems, I never had the intention of sharing them with anyone else. However, I've come to the realization that they can be useful to others. These poems can serve as a window which a reader can look through and get a glimpse of what it is like being a teenager with bipolar disorder.

If a person feels they have no hope left, it is because they have buried it deep within themselves. Something must be done to help them regain their hope. I used writing to do this. My writing allowed me to reach out to the people around me, my family, teachers, and friends. They gave me the inspiration, strength, and courage to fight for life. Perhaps, all a person needs is to be reminded there is hope and there are people who care.

If I were to leave you, as a reader, with a message, it would be: even when it seems there is nothing left in the world and it hurts to keep breathing, know it is possible to make it through. When worse comes to worse, please remember that there are capable doctors willing to help you, and your loved ones, if you are feeling like life is not worth living. You may feel you are alone, but you are never truly alone in the world.

Thank you for reading this collection of poetry. May your continued reading open windows to worlds you didn't imagine possible.

-Kate Ringland

i
build
these
great
buildings
of
power
and
now
i
watch
them
crumble
and
fall
before
my
very
eyes

# Junior Year

Imagination is my temple
Color my monks
Stars my spirit
Music my soul
~

Powerful moonlight, you are silent and beautiful

Do your rays burn like the sun's or are they as cold as ice when one draws near?

I fear to come too close lest I find the answer painful.

When your brilliance shines my way I yearn to dance throughout your mystical light.

I look up and imagine if you see me or hear my fervent call you may let me dance among your beams.

I reach high to touch the stars but clouds drift in my way.

I look again, are my feet still grounded?

Am I living in the clouds?

Moon, if you could speak to me, reach through silence, would you?

Or would you, oh beautiful and powerful Moon, embrace the silence, leaving the curious empty?

Moonlight, I would be lost forever without your sparkling being.

Hopefully I am not forgotten and forsaken.

Can only the moon say?

~

Tears of Emptiness
flood the valley behind me
create the waterfall
I tumble down
branches I could grab rush past
sucked under
gasp for air
swallow the salty waters
The Imaginary Friend
sticks his hand in the frozen water
pulls me out
wraps me in a blanket
hugs me close

and

never

lets

go

~

Heart pierced by many arrows
Singing its silent song
Crying in the dark
Seeking the brightness

Withering and dying
Screaming and crying
Waiting and watching
Hoping and wishing

Heart pierced by many arrows
Can no one see?
Alone and in pain
Singing its silent song

~

I'm alone
I'm afraid
I'm waiting
I'm hoping
I'm crying
I'm screaming
I'm stupid
I'm scared
I'm shy
I'm hoping…
~

I am captured by your eyes
Trapped in the deep, darkness
Then you saw my eyes longing for what they can't have

I don't fall into your eyes now
My sanctuary, the cooling abyss is lost to me forever

If you looked now, what is it you would see?
Eyes darkened by years, dulled by exhaustion, and pained by loss
∼

Strange it is to be this way
Alone and in the dark
The fear inside me grows
As moments pass
I lose my way
I hit the wall
Banging hard with my fists
I scream at the bloody wall
The wall does not move
It will not move
I grow weary of impossibility
I lay down on the floor
Sticky and wet
It is cool
Eternity passes, I am on the cool, damp floor
I call out your name in a whisper
The echo is loud and clear
Throbbing painfully in my ears and cutting
Deep into my heart
For the echo is all I hear

~

Don't fall now
The heavens will open up
Swallow you

Don't fall now
The seas will rise
Sweeping you closer to the heavens

Don't fall now
The land will crack and burn
Pushing you toward the sea

Fall now
You can't see land
Cold and uninviting

~

The world has gone
Only stars are left
Shining and bright
The world has gone
Leaving me the biggest thing in the
Universe
The world has gone
I reach for the twinkling brilliance
I can touch
But the world has gone
I do not feel
What is touch without feeling

~

Am I dying inside or is it just me coming alive?
My stomach's in knots.  I throw myself in.
Is that me moving or is the floor starting to spin?
I'm shivering, but my head is on fire.
I could stand here forever staring at the reflection of me.
I could care less about who it is I see.
But I see what they see, and I can't see the hole I feel inside of me.
I try to escape, but the pain, it follows me.
It is all stuck inside me, bursting to get free.
I fear you, but even more so, I fear me.
Silence is not my enemy.
I'm lost inside the void of eternity, but I can finally say
I am happy here, here with me.

~

I can't write this down anymore
Reality has faded away, you are no longer a
Source of hopes, for you have become a dream
When I reach, I fall, I drown in this, this sea imaginary
If I write this forever, I know I'd soon fade,
I would become a ghostly presence of who was once me
And you, you would become as transparent as the sky
I can't do this anymore
Pretend to live a different life, a life with some joy.
Pretend you care even an ounce about who I am
No more metaphors. No more games
The truth has extinguished everything
I write this with no tears this time, no
Stabbing pains of darkness
You are a real person, I commend you for that
It isn't lonely to play the ghost now, just difficult to get by
I can't write this anymore
This subject has run itself out
No doubt, tomorrow will bring a new topic
But you don't need to hear it, you've already
Heard all my soul

~

# Senior Year

I'm disappointed in me.
Disappointed with reality.
Why is it I can't do right?
I feel so alone.
So very empty and alone.

~

Let me alone, ghost that haunts me
Free me from your icy cold grasp
The more I move the tighter your grip
You hurt my inner most core
You show me a pain I don't want
You tempt me, but I try to be loose
Go now, be gone
I don't need you, I have me

~

The crows, They come
One by one
Pick me apart,
Spit me out when They're Done
~

I am floating
The air is free
The fog is gone
I am frightened
There is a tremble deep within
But the smile will not fade from my face
I am happy
The ceiling is lifted
A laugh bubbles
Pure ecstasy

~

I look ahead of me and see I've painted my finger nails black
I'm pushing at this wall I built, a defense against myself
It doesn't move
I turn away from the wall to find a box around me
I've trapped myself
Now the world, when they see me, they'll see this box around me
I run around and around searching for the door
How can I let my friends in? I've trapped them out.
I look up and see my best friend trying to get in to me
She is stopped by barbed wire
She yells out to me "These walls are thin, just kick them down!"
I look to where my feet should be, but I seemed to have cut my legs off
I fall to the dirt and drag myself along the ground
Holy shit, there's a huge pit
I slip along the ground, grabbing at nothing, trying not to fall

~

Don't follow me
Down this road I've laid
Don't follow me
I have paid
You don't want to be here with me
I repeat the cycle
Don't follow me
I can't find my way back again
Don't want to follow me
I can't even see
Please don't follow me!
I think the sun is blinding me

~

Let me release this poison
It's building up inside of me
Just stop and listen to me
This acid I think
It's burning a hole straight through me
I need to get out
~

If I had words to describe this pain
I'd tell you instantly
I don't have any words
They just don't cut it
I'm stuck in hell
And I thought telling you
Would break the spell
But you just stare blankly
Looking the other way
I think that's ok
Just let me say I'm sorry
I know it doesn't help
But I don't think anything can help me now

~

I can't tell you how your look fills me with dread
It makes me want to take back everything I've said
I am truly me and you are truly you
If only you could see the way I--
The darkness is endless now
Your face is here to fill the emptiness
I only scream because I know too much and I've said too much
I am truly me and you can only be truly you
If only you could see the way I—
Here I am again filling these pages with hollow wisdom
You consume me and maybe that's why I wish I could hate you

~

Why shouldn't this fire consume me?
Burn me through and never be done
I tried to escape its wrath once
I wanted to relieve my tired self from this agony
But it won't let me go
But why shouldn't I let it hold me
I love this warmth and innocence
Why shouldn't I let this angry fire eat me alive

~

I push it deeper,
The knife sticking out of me
I ask for this pain,
If it lets you know I'm still here
I haven't faded
Into the black of the background
You ignore me
While I ignore you
But I know you have seen
Who I could be
I won't let anyone
Else see
This is just you and me

~

The stars collide again tonight
And here I am getting ready to make flight
I don't want to be in this place anymore,
This hell my mind has created.
The star shines most brilliantly just before it dies
I reach my soul out to the skies
Pleading for this pain to go away
But without the pain, how would we know we are alive.
~

Let it all fall down

Let it break away

I never did trust you to save the day

The screams you hear

Aren't yours, but mine

Without the will to go on

I'm just singing that same old song

Hear me. Hear me!

Just don't fear me

~

Let it pass, this demon that haunts me
Banish it to the depths of hell where it belongs
Don't let it drag me down again
I fear that next time it will destroy me
Let the demon burst into flames
And let the moon sing to me again
I don't want to hear the screaming anymore
Give it up, the demon that kills all, but one emotion
Let it die so I may live

~

Don't cry anymore
You're the only one that ever saw me
And the only one that ever will
It's cold in this world of invisibility
But don't cry anymore
There's a loneliness here that no space can fill
Don't bother to care
Who needs to acknowledge the psycho's presence
I don't mind being the shadow that briefly has life
On the wall of your mind
Don't cry anymore
I see you prove you can't see me
Just the shadow on the wall of your mind
Don't cry anymore
What the hell is wrong with you
I am not a shadow
I am a person
A person with more feelings than they can fathom
Don't cry anymore
Or maybe you never did

~

I am the shadow on the wall in your mind
I am the one gallantly dancing across the brick
But the shadow you see, it can't possibly be all of me
I have faded into nothing
Becoming the invisible, the ignored, and the tormented
I am the shadow
On the wall
In your mind.

~

I hope you're there, you're there to see
Me
When I pass from this reality
I'm gone already
There are clouds in my head
I'm lying here, all alone
Lost in a world I can only call my own
No one wants to know or wants to see
What has really gone and happened to me

~

Fall down
Hide away
Feel this now
Die away
Fade to nothing
Have no reason
Touch the cold
Slip away
Darkness envelopes
Scream away
Chill down the spine
Hear no sound
Feel no pain

~

The monster comes with horn and fang
Comes to bring its doom
Tears at flesh, rips from bone
But leaves no trace when it's done
The monster has gone now
You think I remain
Not likely
This is just a vessel full to the brim with pain
~

Let it consume
This that eats away at me
I can't stand this life anymore
The hours pass too slowly
Lethargy making days seem like years
Screaming in my head
I can't make the sound stop
The fire is burning black
Burning cold and alone
The pain starts within me
Nothing I do will cut it out
Let it all consume me
I close my eyes and float away
I cease to be a part of this reality

~

hysteria

I see stars
Swirling, twirling, falling, rising
Bright and shining, they surround me
I reach up my hand
I can touch the stars
Gentle and calming, the stars give to me some of their positive energy
The energy fills my body, my soul
I am bright and shiny
Swirling, twirling, falling, rising
~

I am the lone ranger
Free from all responsibility
Not a care in the world for others
I am the independent
I am the leader of my own club
Where the only member is me
No one would miss me if were to walk away
I am alone
I hate
Being me
~

I am dying one day at a time,
No one really wants to know that.
I am crying a minute at a time,
But I don't need you to know that.
I don't want you to fear me,
My eyes are the only part of me that still has strength to love.
Is my smile big enough to see,
A meager veil for my torrent of tears.
If the sun prepares to shine,
I will no longer fear change.
I know it is coming,
Maybe tomorrow will be ok.
Just tell me everything is going to be ok.

~

Welcome to Hell.

They don't know
How I've dreamed of being one of them
They don't care
How long I've tried to be a part of them
They are here
How could they see me in front of them
They are gone
How lonely it is outside of them

~

I feel the snores of the slumbering demon
I shudder because I feel it--

There!

It's only a matter of time
Until this demon wakes
Every time it rises
With fresh fury

The demon consumes me
It's fire swallows me
Now where shall I go

With demon in lead
It takes me to the tallest mountain
Only to throw me off
So I sit and shudder

I fear the demon's waking

~

I live on H Street
In the town called
Nowhere
I crawl to school everyday
Where we sit and do
Nothing
I dream up my empty plans
They are full, full of
No one
Who will come and take me
Away
But none of those details matter
As long as you tell me everything's
Going to be
OK

~

I'm lost again
I can't seem to find reality
I stare into the void
I don't know what I really see
Your blank face stares back at me
I can't remember your smile
The smile you gave to me
I'm crying now
I've totally lost control
All I ask of you
No, All I ask of me
Please, don't fall too hard again
This concrete may kill me
You are far away
But you were so close
And I slammed the door shut
Did you even know it was me
~

Red and blue
Stars burn through their existence
Back and forth
Ripples on a pond
Somehow this quiets us
Giving us the answers
Even though there were no questions

~

What frees my emotions
What keeps me sane
What it is I do solely for myself
What allows me to stay grounded in reality
What voices my fears
What echoes my thoughts
What aides my horrible memory
What lets loose my wild imagination
What is writing

~

tomorrow seems possible
i find the darkness does not encompass me
i keep running only to find
i am standing still
your smile warms my tortured soul
you inspire me
hope fills me with dread
was there a mistake
and i will truly fall to my doom
and darkness
i can only believe
tomorrow will be ok

~

About the Authors

 Kate Ringland is currently attending the University of Washington as a Psychology Major. Her aspiration is to one day become librarian and spend her entire day surrounded by books. She has been writing as a hobby since before she could write and plans on continuing to write into her senility. She lives in Seattle, Washington with her cats, Punk and Aggie, and her bird, Arika. Her other current project is a fictional fantasy novel.

 Ellie Ringland lives in Troutdale, Oregon where she is currently enrolled in a GED program. After completion of the program, she plans on traveling and later attending an out-of-state college. She has been writing poetry most of her life and plans on continuing for the remainder of it.

Further Resources

Depression and Bipolar Support Alliance

    http://www.dbsalliance.org/

National Alliance of Mental Illness

    http://www.nami.org/

Anxiety Disorders Association of America

    http://www.adaa.org/

Focus Adolescent Services

    http://www.focusas.com/index.html

www.ingramcontent.com/pod-product-compliance
Lightning Source LLC
Chambersburg PA
CBHW031413040426
42444CB00005B/542